Cook Lionfish

Claire Wood & Polly Alford

with

Lionfish University

Revised Edition

A portion of the proceeds from the sale of this cookbook will go to help our ocean conservation efforts at Lionfish University, a 501c3 non-profit.

Lionfish invasion in the Mediterranean Sea!

Author: **Aylin Ulman PhD**
Founder: **Mersea Marine Conservation Consulting, Fethiye, Turkey**

The invasive lionfish problem in the Western Atlantic (east coast of the United States, Caribbean Sea and Gulf of Mexico) is known to be the most problematic and disastrous marine invasion in history! To make matters worse, the lionfish problem has recently spread to the Mediterranean!

In 2012, two lionfish specimens (Pterois miles) were caught off Lebanon. Since then, they have been rapidly spreading throughout the Eastern Mediterranean. By 2013, they reached Turkey and Cyprus and by 2015 they made it to Rhodes Island in Greece and also all the way to Tunisian waters in the Central Mediterranean Sea. By 2016, they were reported in Sicily and by 2019 they reached Malta and Libya.

Lionfish are native to the Indo-Pacific region and the Red Sea. They most likely entered the Mediterranean through the Suez Canal, and thus can be called 'Lessepsian migrants', named after the French developer of the Suez Canal, which artificially joins the Red Sea with the Mediterranean.

The Eastern Mediterranean is extremely low in nutrients such as phosphate, a necessary building block needed to support

A school of lionfish in Bodrum, Turkey, July 2019, just one month after the first record was reported there.

life. Therefore, naturally there is much less life there to begin with. Also, it is extremely overfished and hence almost devoid of larger predatory fish which are important components providing ecosystem control and regulation. Additionally, due to its proximity to the Suez Canal, it is continually invaded by new Indo-Pacific species, making it the most invaded sea on the planet! Alien species are now much more common than native species in the countries closest to the Suez Canal such as Israel, Cyprus, Lebanon, Turkey and parts of Greece. With the lack of larger fish predominantly due to over fishing, there are niches left to fill for these new species, many of which are very successful! Especially as the Mediterranean continues to warm, making it more akin to Red Sea temperatures!

Scientists are striving to understand why lionfish populations are controlled in their native range, but increase exponentially in invaded habitats? Possible hypotheses likely include a combination of the following: a scarcity of natural predators, prey naiveté (their targeted prey not yet having learned that lionfish are predators), young maturity, high reproduction, voracious appetites, together with warming seas. A dusky grouper was recently witnessed eating a lionfish in Turkey, providing the first evidence of natural predation in the Mediterranean. However, groupers are overfished in the Mediterranean, therefore their predation alone will unlikely translate into an effective form of natural control.

Marine invasive species are almost impossible to eradicate once established! Therefore, we fully advocate culling programs to try to control the explosion. If the Mediterranean invasion is half as horrific as the Atlantic Belt and the Caribbean and lionfish reproduce in the Mediterranean non-stop, it is feared they will help decimate what remains of native biodiversity. Thus, adding further damage to the marine fisheries, which have been declining for decades. In fact, many small-scale fishers in the region can no longer meet their operating costs due to declining catches and are sadly quitting the profession altogether.

Initially, scuba divers in the Eastern Mediterranean were excited to see this new colorful fish swimming around this rather bland seascape and were apprehensive about killing them. However, most scuba divers are avid conservationists and their support is now being sought to spear and remove lionfish to help control the early stages of this invasion.

One positive thing about lionfish is that after removing their spines, they are safe to eat and delicious with their slight buttery flavor. The best way to deal with this new invader is to get them from the sea to the plate. This wonderful cookbook will surely help with that!

Our story

In 2003, Polly Alford founded Reef Conservation International (ReefCI). A non-profit marine conservation organization. Through tourism, ReefCI focuses on the general health of the coral reefs and commercial species in Southern Belize.

During 2009, ReefCI introduced a Lionfish program. The initiative concentrated on removing, dissecting and collecting lionfish data. Together with helping to create awareness and vertical markets. The program became the primary project. 7 years later, the same organization removed over 7,000 lionfish!

The initiative helped Belize create a culture that placed a value on lionfish. In the beginning, the general consensus in Belize was that lionfish were poisonous and people were afraid to eat it!

Spreading awareness through social media, booths at events and, guests ReefCI helped change that perception. Every week Polly did a presentation about lionfish to an average of 14 people on visiting sailboats. And, they were served tasty lionfish dishes.

When the guests asked what they could do to help, Polly suggested that when they return to the Belize mainland, they ask for lionfish in restaurants. This helped create a demand! If there is a desire to eat a particular fish at restaurants, a market is created for fishermen.

Restaurants are now serving lionfish in Belize and fisherman are being paid a high dollar value per pound. Polly got invited to San Andres, Colombia to talk at a Forum of Sustainable Tourism on Small Islands.

"Belize is a model for us in conservation and environmental protection, especially in the application of lionfish population and strategies. We could not find a better example of that than what you guys are doing at ReefCI in Belize"

Claire

Claire Wood is a caterer and chef, she has owned cafes and restaurants in Tunbridge Wells and Brighton, South East England. She currently operates Souper Juice cafe and an events catering business, in Tunbridge Wells, Kent.

Polly

In 2003, Polly left her UK Corporate world to set up a Marine Conservation organization in Belize. Polly still lives in Placencia, Southern Belize with her Belizean husband, Roland. She continues to focus on marine conservation, in particular the lionfish problem. Polly & Roland operate a deep-sea fishing and diving business, Blue Reef Adventures.

In 2018 Polly and Claire met Stacy Frank and Jim Hart, co-founders of the marine conservation non-profit, Lionfish University. Their mutual missions to save the reefs from invasive lionfish inspired their collaboration to get the message out that the destructive invasive lionfish are good to eat. "Eat 'em to beat 'em", "Kill 'em and grill 'em" and "Take a Lionfish to Lunch and … Eat It!" are just some of the phrases promoting lionfish as a healthy food source.

Lionfish University provides a forum for divers and ocean conservationists dedicated to the preservation of our oceans' reefs and native fish populations being threatened by the lionfish invasion spreading throughout the Caribbean, the Gulf of Mexico, the Western Atlantic, and down to South America. The founders launched this non-profit (501c3) as a grassroots effort in 2012 to share information and resources relating to the infestation of this invasive species, and to support research in lionfish control and removal.

The goal of Lionfish University is to promote community efforts and scientific research to curb lionfish populations, to raise awareness in the global community about the importance of maintaining the fragile ecosystem that invasive lionfish continue to threaten, and to promote lionfish as a viable, healthy, tasty food source.

Lionfish University Founders

Stacy Frank
Stacy has been an avid scuba diver since 1973, and she lives to dive. She has a master's degree in Industrial and Organizational Psychology, and lives in Ashville, North Carolina with her husband, Dr. Barry Frank. It became clear during research for a lionfish thriller screenplay that our Caribbean reefs are being threatened by many factors, including the invasive Indo-Pacific lionfish, and that now is the time to face the nemesis.

Courtney Platt
Courtney is a Caymanian professional photographer who has made over 5,000 dives in Grand Cayman since 1983. He is a personal witness to the devastating effect that over-fishing has had on diving tourism, and now made worse by the invasive lionfish. He is an ardent proponent of reversing these destructive trends to help the recovery of native reef fish populations.

Jim Hart
Jim is a diving addicted screenwriter with numerous writing and producing credits including Hook!, Bram Stoker's Dracula, Contact, Sahara, August Rush, Epic, Crossbones and others. While working on a lionfish thriller screenplay he became interested in the geo-political impact that lionfish are having on reef systems and people in the small island nations of the Caribbean. Hart lives in NYC when he is not diving.

Credits

Photography – James Travis
www.travisdigital.co.uk
Logo & Book Design– Jim Clarkson
www.jimdesign.co.uk

Lionfish à la Monica

Serves 4

For the lionfish
2 lbs lionfish
½ tsp kosher salt
½ tsp ground black pepper
virgin olive oil

For the salsa
2 tbsp virgin olive oil
1 cup cherry tomatoes (halved or quartered)
¼ cup fresh basil
4-6 shallots

For the herb crush
¾ cup bread crumbs
¾ cup parmesan cheese
½ cup fresh parsley

For the vegetable
1 lb butternut squash
1 tsp salt
1 tsp ground black pepper
3 tbsp virgin olive oil

Garnish
virgin olive oil and balsamic vinegar to drizzle on plates

Monica Archer, private chef in Antigua, prepares her original recipe, Lionfish à la Monica, for the first time and talks about it on Antigua/Barbuda TV.

Lionfish
Preheat oven to 400°F.
Season lionfish with salt and black pepper and drizzle a little olive oil over, leave to marinate for about 1 hour.
Heat olive oil in a pan over medium to high heat. Add lionfish and sear on both sides; don't cook through.

Salsa
In a medium-hot pan with 2 tbsp olive oil add cherry tomatoes, shallots, salt and black pepper for a couple of minutes then take off heat.

Herb crush
Blend parsley, parmesan cheese and bread crumbs.

Vegetable
Peel butternut squash, cut into 2 inch cubes and add salt, black pepper, drizzle with oil and bake in oven for about 40 min.

Cover fish with butternut squash and salsa, top with herb crush, finish fish in oven for 5 min.

Drizzle plates with balsamic vinegar and olive oil for garnish.

In April, 2019 Lionfish University and our science team visited the island of Antigua at the request of Martha Watkins Gilkes and the Mill Reef Club to assess the damage to the reefs from invasive lionfish. One of the solutions to these pesky invaders is to Take A Lionfish to Lunch … And Eat It!!!! Go Green … Eat Red Lionfish!!!! Antiguan Chef Monica Archer made this recipe on her very first try at cooking invasive lionfish and it was a hit!! Here seen on Antigua and Barbuda Broadcasting Services TV (ABS).

1 Using a sharp filet knife, holding the head of the lionfish with your other hand, make a vertical incision just below and perpendicular to the head. Push down hard with the knife and slice the meat from the bone, keeping the knife close to the bone.

2 Do not remove the filet from the carcass.

3 Place your hand just above the filet near the tail, apply pressure and push down hard with the knife to remove the filet.

4 Feel for the rib cage and slice off the edge.

5 On the side of the removed rib cage, cut a small triangle to remove the bone. Turn the fish over and repeat steps 1-5.

Why Cook Lionfish?

Lionfish are native to the Pacific, Indian Ocean and the Red Sea. Unfortunately, they have found their way into the Atlantic, Gulf of Mexico and Caribbean. Experts believe that the cause of the lionfish invasion was the dumping of unwanted lionfish from aquariums into the Atlantic. Lionfish have now invaded the Mediterranean likely through the Suez Canal.

Invasive lionfish have few natural predators and they are ferocious predators. They are a threat to our coral reefs and ecosystems. Vacuum cleaners that suck the life out of the ocean!

They breed rapidly, releasing roughly 30,000 eggs every 2–3 days, and the larvae have few predators!

Lionfish eat juvenile fish and cleaners such as shrimp that reduce external parasites on native reef fish. They are feeding on our key species such as juvenile parrotfish. Algae and coral fight for photosynthesis. The parrotfish help keep the coral alive by feeding on the algae. If the algae smother the reef, the coral will die and there is no chance of recovery.

It is estimated that marine plants produce between 70-80% of the oxygen that we need in order to survive. Without coral reefs, life as we know it cannot exist. The "eat 'em to beat 'em" campaign was launched by the National Oceanic and Atmospheric Administration (NOAA) in 2010 to encourage a seafood market as a means of mitigating the species' impact on reef communities.

In 2003, Polly Alford founded a conservation diving organization in Belize. She encountered her first lionfish in 2009 and was subsequently shocked by the rapid invasion. Her organization introduced a project to remove them, collect data and create local and national awareness.

In 2016 Polly decided to enroll her twin sister, Claire (a chef in the UK) in a project to combine their skills and write a lionfish cookbook. The objective was to write easy to follow recipes using lionfish to create tasty dishes for home cooking.

The recipes in this book demonstrate the versatility of this fish. Lionfish is delicious and is high in healthy Omega-3 fatty acids.

We wrote this book to encourage you to cook one of the most sustainable foods available, while helping to reduce this potentially catastrophic environmental problem.

Enjoy!

Brunch

Lionfish Eggs Benedict

Serves 2

For the lionfish
2 lionfish filets
half a stick butter
3 glasses sparkling wine

For the Hollandaise
1 stick melted butter
1 tbsp lemon juice
3 large egg yolks
seasoning

For the poached eggs
4 eggs
2 tsp white vinegar
1 tsp salt

2 English muffins, split

Place the butter and wine in a frying pan, bring to a boil then turn down the heat, place the lionfish in the liquor and gently poach for 2 minutes.

For the hollandaise, melt the butter in the microwave or in a pan, do not let it burn.

Place the egg yolks and lemon juice in a food processor, blend for a couple of minutes then slowly add the melted butter. Season.

Toast the muffins. Bring a pan of water to boil and add the vinegar. Break the eggs into the boiling water, then turn down to a simmer (make sure there is enough water to cover the eggs and that the water is always moving) simmer for 3-4 minutes then remove.

Place the lionfish on top of each muffin, top with the egg then spoon over the hollandaise.

Why are Lionfish a problem?

An average female lionfish can spawn roughly 30,000 eggs every 2–3 days. Year round, close to 4 million eggs! Every female is permanently carrying eggs at some stage of development! The egg sac contains a chemical deterrent that discourages other fish from eating them. They have a high recruitment rate to a suitable habitat, meaning that the eggs have a higher chance of becoming larvae, to grow into juvenile fish that settle where they can live relatively free from environmental pressure.

Lionfish, Quinoa and Chili Omelette
with Cilantro

Serves 1

3 eggs, beaten
handful cilantro leaves
1 chili, chopped
½ cup cooked quinoa
10 oz poached lionfish
vegetable oil
seasoning

Place a non-stick pan on a high heat, then add oil. When oil is nearly smoking discard the oil, then add eggs, moving them around the pan.

When the egg mix is nearly cooked, add the rest of the ingredients. Season and leave for a couple of minutes, then fold and empty onto plate.

Over 42 million people in the Western Atlantic Basin make their living from coral reefs, mainly through fishing and tourism.

Lionfish Frittatas
with Tabbouleh

Serves 2

- 12 oz lionfish
- 1 cup peas
- 3 cups shredded kale
- 1 cup ricotta cheese
- 3 eggs
- 1 tbsp lemon zest
- 2 tbsp mint, chopped
- 1 tbsp parsley, chopped
- vegetable oil
- arugula
- watercress
- olive oil
- tabbouleh (page 73)

Poach lionfish for 2 minutes (until cooked) then drain. Whip the eggs and add the cooked lionfish, peas, kale, cheese, lemon zest, mint and parsley.

Place a frying pan on a medium to high heat with the vegetable oil, drain the oil and spoon patties mix into the pan cooking each one for 2-3 minutes on each side, add more oil if you need to.

Serve with a mix of watercress and arugula a drizzle of olive oil and Tabbouleh.

A single Lionfish may reduce the number of juvenile native fish by approximately 80% in just 5 weeks!

Data collected are showing that lionfish will eat anything that they can fit into their mouths. Their stomach can expand up to 30 times the normal volume and a lionfish will fill it up to capacity as soon as it is able! Through stomach content analysis, scientists have catalogued over 167 vertebrate and invertebrate species that lionfish will eat. This includes fish they eat plus shrimp, crabs, juvenile octopus, squid and juvenile lobster.

Photo Credit: Courtney Platt Photography

Appetizers

Lionfish Spring Rolls
with Mango Salad and Hot Sauce

Serves 6

for the spring rolls
½ lb lime pickled lionfish, chopped
2 tbsp spring onion, chopped
3 tbsp mooli, chopped
1 tbsp cilantro, chopped
lemon juice, soy sauce, oyster sauce to taste
12 sheets filo pastry
vegetable oil for deep frying

for the salad
2 large mangos, diced
1 red chili, finely chopped
7oz baby spinach
1 large avocado, diced
2 fl oz soy sauce
2 fl oz vegetable oil
1 tsp honey

For the Spring Rolls
Mix all the ingredients into a bowl (excluding the pastry and the oil), adding the lemon juice, soy sauce and oyster sauce to taste.
Lay the pastry sheets on a clean work surface. Spread one twelfth of the filling at one end of the pastry, and gently roll tucking in the edges. Repeat with the remaining pastry.
Preheat the oil in a deep fat fryer to 350°F. Deep fry each roll until crisp and golden. Carefully remove and transfer to a plate lined with paper towels.

For the Salad
Place the soy sauce, honey and oil in a bowl. Whisk a little then fold in the other ingredients. Serve with Hot Sauce (p73).

While the lionfish is eating, its stomach can expand 30 times normal size. They are the buffet busters of the reef!

Butternut Squash and Green Chili Soup

with Lionfish Ceviche

Serves 4

2 butternut squash, peeled and diced
1 small white onion, diced
2 green chilies, sliced
1 tbsp vegetable oil
16 oz water
1 can coconut milk
4 large spoonfuls of lionfish ceviche (page 33)

Preheat the oven to 400°F. Place the squash on an oven tray, sprinkle with oil and seasoning and roast for 20-30 minutes until tender.
Saute the onion and chilies in a heavy bottomed saucepan until soft. Add cooked squash and cover with water, bringing to a boil and simmer for 10 minutes. Blend the soup, add the coconut milk, check the seasoning and add a large spoonful of lionfish ceviche to serve.

Lionfish have 18 venomous spines and once snipped off they are just like any other fish to prepare to eat. Lionfish are not poisonous!

Lionfish Salad with Lychee and Chili

1 tbsp fish sauce
1 tsp superfine sugar
1 lb lionfish filet
1 tbsp vegetable oil
½ sweet red pepper, cut into strips
5 lychees, peeled and deseeded or a small tin of lychees, drained
handful cilantro leaves
1 long red chili, deseeded and julienned
5 baby tomatoes, sliced in halves
1 small bag mixed lettuce
2 tbsp lime juice
2 tbsp olive oil
1 tsp chili flakes

Squeeze out any excess water from the lionfish in paper towels.
Marinate the lionfish filets in the fish sauce and 1 tsp of superfine sugar. Cover and place in fridge for 10 minutes.
Arrange the lettuce, sweet pepper, tomatoes and lychee on a small platter. Heat the vegetable oil in a non-stick pan over medium to high heat. Cook the lionfish for a minute or until cooked.
Mix the lime juice and olive and season with a pinch of salt and pepper. Scatter the lionfish over the salad. Drizzle the dressing over the top, sprinkle with chili flakes and serve immediately.

Lionfish Straws

Serves 2

6 lionfish filets
7 fl oz vegetable oil
7oz all purpose flour
7oz rice flour
1 lemon, zest (keep juice for lemon mayonnaise)
12 fl oz beer
rock salt and black pepper

Cut fish into 3-4 inch strips lengthwise. Place on paper towels to absorb any moisture.
For the batter, whisk together both flours with the lemon zest then add the beer, whisking constantly.
Pour the oil in a heavy based pan and heat until a drop of batter sizzles and browns. Dip fish strips into the batter, coating evenly. Place them in the hot oil and cook them for about 4 minutes until they are golden brown. Season well with the salt and pepper and serve with chili sauce or lemon mayonnaise.

Lime Marinated Lionfish Salad

Serves 4

1 lb lionfish, filets, diced
4 limes — juice of
1 tsp garlic paste
1 red onion, halved and thinly sliced
2 birdseye (or any hot) chilies, finely chopped
5 tbsp white wine vinegar
¾ cup vegetable oil
large handful arugla lettuce
handful cilantro leaves, coarsely chopped
1 mango, diced

Marinate the fish in the lime, set aside.

Place the garlic, vinegar, oil in a bowl and whisk lightly. Toss in all the other ingredients including the marinated fish and serve.

Hudut-traditional Garifuna Meal

Serves 4

Sere is the Garifuna name for the soup

1½ lbs lionfish filet
1 onion sliced and cut in half
4 cloves minced garlic
4 tbsp coconut oil / cooking oil
2 cans coconut milk
3 cups water
2 tsp salt
1 tsp black pepper
1 whole habanero pepper without seeds (optional)
spices desired
2 green plantains
2 half ripe plantains
8 cups water
½ tsp salt
¼ cup sere

Directions: Sere

Clean, core, and season fish with the salt and pepper and set aside. Heat the coconut oil in pot and add onions and garlic along with desired seasoning—including salt and black Pepper. Saute for a few minutes and add the coconut milk and water. Let sit for a few minutes until it starts heating up. At this point you will constantly need to use spoon to stir milk. Stir constantly with spoon. The milk will start to curdle if you do not maintain the constant motion. Add fish. Remove fish after about 5 minutes and put to one side. Let the soup continue boiling and bubble until the soup is thickened. Taste for flavor, add salt and pepper to taste. 5 minutes before you turn off the stove, add the Habanero Pepper to the soup—ensure the pepper is whole and do not break open. After soup is thickened remove ¼ cup and add to the plantains in the food processor.

Directions: Hudut
Peel and cut plantains. Each plantain should be cut in three or four pieces. Boil plantains in 8 cups of water. After they are half way done, add the half ripe plantains. Let all plantains boil until they are fully cooked. Remove from water and put them in the food processor. Let them cool a little before processing. You will need to process after Sere is made because you will need ¼ cup of Sere to add to plantains before processing. Pulse until it is the consistency you prefer.

Heat the soup. Add a rough ball of Hudut and put the lionfish back into the dish prior to serving.

Happy Garifuna meal!

Quinoa and Lionfish Solterito

Serves 4 (appetizer)

⅓ cups red & white quinoa, cooked
¾ cup corn kernels cooked
1 lb lionfish roughly diced
(marinated in lime for 30 minutes to cook)
¾ cup fava beans, cooked
1 small onion, finely diced
2 chilies, finely diced
handful parsley, chopped
4 tbsp white wine vinegar
5 tbsp vegetable oil
2 cloves garlic, crushed
handful mint leaves, chopped

Lightly whisk the vinegar, oil and garlic. Add all the other ingredients and serve.

Solterito is a Peruvian appetizer, always served cold.

Smoked Haddock, Lionfish, Spinach & Bacon Chowder

Serves 8

1 tbsp vegetable oil
1 onion, diced
4 oz smoked bacon, diced
1 lb lionfish filets, cut into chunks
1 lb undyed smoked haddock, skinned, pinned and cut into chunks
40 fl oz double cream
15 fl oz full fat milk
6 medium potatoes, peeled & diced
5 oz fresh spinach

Sweat onions and bacon with the oil in a large saucepan until the bacon is cooked and the onions are soft.
Add the diced potatoes, cream and milk. Bring to a boil and simmer for about 30 minutes or until the potatoes are soft.
Add the smoked haddock; simmer for 5 minutes, add lionfish and simmer for another 5 minutes. Stir in the spinach until wilted and serve.

Lionfish and Wasabi Croquettes

Serves 4

½ lb lionfish filets
1 15 oz can chickpeas, drained and rinsed
1 shallot, finely diced
1 tbsp fresh white breadcrumbs
2 tbsp natural yogurt
2 tbsp wasabi paste
2-3 tbsp butter, melted
freshly ground black pepper
1-2 medium eggs
7 oz chopped hazlenuts
flour for dusting

Roughly chop the lionfish and cover with boiling water. Leave for 5 minutes, drain. Place the fish, chickpeas, breadcrumbs, shallot, wasabi, yogurt, and melted butter in a food processor and blitz to a smooth thick paste (if it's too thick add more yogurt, if it's too thin add more breadcrumbs).
Divide the mixture into 12 equal portions and roll into even patties. Place the beaten eggs and hazelnuts into separate bowls. Roll the croquettes first in flour, then in the egg mix and then in the chopped hazelnuts, to coat them evenly on all sides.
In a heavy based saucepan over moderate heat, preheat at least 2 inches of oil to 350. Deep fry the croquettes, a few at a time, in the hot oil for 6-8 minutes until golden brown. Transfer them to paper towels to remove any excess oil..
Serve with crisp salad leaves and a lemon crème fraiche.

Lime Marinated Lionfish Salad
with Tomatoes, Avocado, Cucumber and Chipotle

Serves 4

1 lb lionfish filets
4 limes—juice of
½ cucumber, seeded and diced
1 pint cherry tomatoes, halved
1 avocado, cut into chunks
olive oil
2 limes, quartered
seasoning
chipotle sauce (page 73)

Place the fish filets in the lime juice and marinate for 10 minutes. In a bowl, place the tomatoes, cucumber and avocado. Mix and drizzle with olive oil, divide onto serving plates. In a medium hot pan flash fry the fish and place on top of the salads. Serve with chipotle sauce.

Lionfish with Sweet Potato Toast, Avocado and Cilantro & Lime Crème Fraiche

Serves 2

8 lionfish filets
2 x ¼ inch slices of sweet potato
1 ripe avocado
4 fl oz crème fraiche
tsp cilantro, chopped
1 lime — juice of
olive oil
seasoning

Preheat the oven to 400°F.
Drizzle the sweet potato slices with oil and seasoning. Bake in the oven 10 minutes until cooked. Spread the avocado flesh over the potatoes. In a skillet, pan fry the fish over medium heat for 1-2 minutes each side. In a bowl, mix the lime, cilantro and crème fraiche. Place the fish on top of the avocado and spoon over the crème fraiche.

Lionfish Wrapped in Parma Ham Stuffed with Mozzarella on Pesto Toast

Serves 4

8 lionfish filets
4 slices parma ham
1 ball baby mozzarella
4 slices sourdough bread
pesto dressing (page 73)

Preheat the oven to 350°F.

Pound the fish and place each one on a parma ham slice. Divide the mozzarella ball into 4 pieces and place on the fish. Wrap the fish and ham around the mozzarella into a ball.

Bake in oven for 15 minutes. Drizzle the pesto over the bread slices and place in oven for 10 minutes until they have toasted. Serve the parma ham balls on the toasts.

Lionfish Wontons with Sweet Chili and Soy Sauce

Serves 4

8 chinese cabbage leaves
1 pound chopped lionfish filets
2 spring onions, finely chopped
1 handful cilantro leaves, chopped
1 inch ginger, peeled and grated
½ tsp sugar
1 tbsp sesame oil
seasoning
1 egg, beaten plus 1 egg white
16 wonton wrappers
3 cups vegetable oil

sweet chili sauce (page 73)

Bring a pan of water to boil, add cabbage and cook until tender, drain, coarsely chop and set aside.
Place fish in a bowl, add onions, cabbage, cilantro, ginger, sugar and sesame oil, season and mix. Add egg white and mix again.
Lay wonton wrappers on a clean work counter. Place a little filling in the centre of each wrapper, brush the edges with beaten egg and fold into triangle shape, bringing the points of the triangle together to finish.
Heat the vegetable oil in a large pan to 350°F.
Drop wontons carefully into oil and cook for 6-8 minutes until crispy, drain on paper towels and serve.

Pea and Mint Soup
with Crispy Lionfish

Serves 4

1 onion sliced
splash vegetable oil
10 oz frozen peas
good handful of fresh mint leaves
34 fl oz water
8 lionfish filets
3 fl oz vegetable oil
3 oz self-rising flour
3 oz rice flour
1 lemon zest, grated
5 fl oz beer
rock salt and black pepper

Sweat onion and peas in oil until the peas are defrosted, add water and bring to a boil. Immediately add mint, blend and season to taste
Cut fish into thin strips lengthways, lay on paper towels to absorb any moisture.

To make the batter, place both flours in a bowl with the lemon zest, whisk the dry ingredients then add the beer, slowly whisking all the time.
Place the oil in a heavy based pan and heat until a drop of batter sizzles and browns. Dip the strips of fish into the batter making sure they are evenly coated then place them in the hot oil and cook them for about 2 minutes until they are golden brown. Season well with the salt and pepper and serve on top of the soup.

Lionfish Pate

Serves 4

1 lb lionfish filets
4 limes — juice of
7 oz cream cheese
1 lemon — juice of
handful fresh chervil
2 tsp wasabi paste

Marinate the fish in the lime juice for about half an hour to cook. Place the fish with the lime juice, lemon juice, cream cheese, wasabi and half the chervil leaves in a food processor and blend until smooth.
Serve with toasted sourdough and garnish with the rest of the chervil.

1lb lionfish filets
1 onion, diced
2 cloves garlic, chopped
2-3 tbsp ginger, chopped
1 lb mushrooms, sliced
14 oz carrots, peeled and sliced
1 lb red peppers, sliced
3 red chilies, chopped
7 oz green beans
8 oz jar green chili paste
50 fl oz fish stock
2 cans coconut milk
bunch cilantro leaves

Thai Vegetable Soup with Lionfish

Serves 6

In a large pan, sweat onion, mushrooms, carrots and peppers until the mushrooms are cooked. Add the garlic, chili, ginger and curry paste.

Pour in the stock and bring to a boil, simmer for 20 minutes then add the coconut milk.
In a skillet, pan fry the lionfish in hot oil for 2-3 minutes. Add the cilantro to the soup, check seasoning and serve. Break up the fish and divide into bowls, garnish with cilantro leaves.

Lionfish, Beetroot, New Potato and Lambs Lettuce Salad
with Horseradish Crème Fraiche

Serves 4

3 lbs lionfish filets, sliced
7 oz crème fraiche
2 tbsp horseradish sauce
5 oz corn salad lettuce or watercress
6 oz beets, cooked and diced
7 oz new potatoes, cooked
olive oil

Mix the horseradish with the crème fraiche, fold in the beets and potatoes. Dust the fish with seasoned flour and fry for 2 minutes on each side.

Divide the lettuce between the plates, drizzle with olive oil, place the potato and beet mix on each plate and top with the lionfish.

Coral reefs and life as we know it could die!

Coral and algae fight for photosynthesis to survive. The grazer fish, such as parrotfish, will feed on the algae. This helps keep coral reefs alive. Now we have lionfish feeding on juvenile parrotfish and other species, fish stocks are reduced AND the health of the coral reefs are in jeopardy! Coral reefs generate as much as 80% of oxygen that we need in order to survive!

The Mesoamerican Reef in Central America is the second largest reef system in the world and the largest barrier reef in the Northern hemisphere. If the reef is smothered and dies under the additional pressures caused by lionfish, what will happen? How will humans and mammals survive without oxygen?

Lionfish
with Ginger, Chili and Spring Onion

Serves 4

8 lionfish cut in half
3 tbsp vegetable oil
2-3 tbsp ginger, finely chopped
3 cloves garlic, finely chopped
3 red chilies, finely sliced
small bunch spring onion, sliced
1 tsp soy sauce

Season fish. Preheat a skillet and add 1 tsp of the oil to the hot pan, fry the fish for 1 minute on each side. Remove from heat and keep warm.

Heat the rest of the oil, and in the same pan, saute the ginger, garlic and chilies until golden, take off the heat and add the onions.

Place the fish on a serving plate, splash the fish with the soy sauce and spoon over the contents of the pan.

Ceviche

Serves 4

1 lb of lionfish filets cut into ½ inch pieces
1 cup fresh lime juice
½ red onion, finely diced
1 cup of chopped fresh tomatoes
1 tsp of salt
1 tsp of season all
1 deseeded habanero pepper, finely chopped
2 tsp of black pepper
1 bunch finely chopped cilantro

tortilla chips
sliced avocado

Note— It is important to try and use the freshest fish and not frozen fish. Do not over marinate this dish. It will make the fish tough!

In a non-reactive dish, mix fish with lime juice and let sit for ½ hour or until the fish turns from pink to white in color.
Mix remaining ingredients into the fish and lime. Mix and cover and refrigerate for an hour.

Serve with fresh tortilla chips and slices of avocado.

Snacks and

Light Meals

Pan-fried Lionfish Sandwich with Pickled Cucumber and Lemon Mayonnaise

Serves 4

4 soft white torpedo rolls
8 lionfish filets
half a cucumber
1 lemon
4 tbsp mayonnaise (page 73)
sea salt
white wine vinegar

Shave the cucumber with a potato peeler discarding the tough skin and seeds. Place in a bowl with a handful of salt. Leave for 5 minutes. Wash salt off then cover with white wine vinegar.
Squeeze lemon juice into the mayonnaise, season.

Pan fry the fish for about 1-2 minutes on each side. Place 2 filets in each bun with the mayonnaise and pickled cucumber.

Lionfish Tacos

Serves: 8 servings (serving size 3 tacos)

3 lbs of fresh lionfish filets
1 tsp of cumin
1 tsp of Old Bay Seasoning
1 tsp of ground cilantro
1 tsp of black pepper
1 tsp of cajun spice
4 cups of shredded red cabbage
4 cups of shredded white cabbage
1 bunch of cilantro
1 diced medium onion
2 cups of diced tomatoes
1 cup of diced fresh pineapple

2 eggs, beaten
1 lb flour
2 quarts vegetable oil for frying

24 corn tortillas

Dressing
1 large tub of plain yogurt
1 finely diced habanero pepper (without seeds)
1 bunch of fresh garden mint, finely chopped
½ cup of lime juice
salt and pepper to taste

Mix red & white cabbage, tomatoes, onion, cilantro and pineapple in a salad bowl. Set aside a handful of red cabbage.

For the dressing, using a blender, finely blend all ingredients.

Mix together cumin, old bay, black pepper, Cajun spice and ground cilantro in a bowl and use the mix to season the whole lionfish filets.

Heat oil in a deep fryer to 365°F. Beat eggs in a bowl. Dredge the lionfish in the egg and then coat with the flour and fry until golden brown. Set fried filets to one side.

Place 3 corn tortillas on each serving plate. Place a handful of vegetable mixture on each tortilla. Place 2 lionfish filets on top of each one. Drizzle with the yogurt dressing and serve with a slice of lime and a sprinkle of red cabbage around each plate for decoration.

Spiced Lionfish Burgers
Serves 4

cajun seasoning (page 73)
8 lionfish filets
4 crispy lettuce leaves
4 large tomato slices

Cilantro Slaw
¼ head green cabbage, thinly sliced
¼ head purple cabbage, thinly sliced
1 small onion, thinly sliced
2 cups mayonnaise (page 73)
½ tsp salt
1 tsp ground black pepper
½ tsp cayenne pepper
2 cups fresh cilantro leaves, barely chopped

4 seeded burger buns

Place the lionfish filets into a bowl, drizzle with vegetable oil and coat with the Cajun seasoning. Preheat a non-stick frying pan, drizzle with vegetable oil and cook lionfish for 1-2 minutes on each side.
For the slaw, place all the ingredients in a bowl and mix well, season to taste.
Assemble burgers by placing lettuce on base of bun, then tomato, fish and slaw, place top of bun on slaw. Serve with fries.

Simple Lionfish Spaghetti
Serves 4

1½ lbs poached lionfish filets (page 10)
2 tbsp olive oil
3-4 garlic cloves, crushed
sea salt
9 oz cherry tomatoes, cut in half
splash dry white wine
handful fresh basil leaves
9 oz spaghetti, cooked al dente, rinsed with cold water in a colander

In a large skillet place the olive oil, and garlic, toss in the white wine, spaghetti, tomatoes and lionfish, heat, add basil and serve with lemon wedges.

Lionfish with Pickled Beets
and Ginger Cabbage
Serves 4

2 lb lionfish filets
4 medium beets, finely sliced
½ head medium green cabbage, finely sliced
1 inch fresh ginger, grated
1 tsp cumin seeds
vegetable oil
seasoning
soy dressing (page 73)

Liberally sprinkle sea salt over the beets and let them marinate for 5-10 minutes. Wash the salt off and cover with white wine vinegar.
In a skillet, fry the cabbage with the ginger and cumin over a medium heat for 15 minutes until tender crisp. Slice half the beets and mix with cabbage.
Dust the fish with seasoned flour and fry for 1-2 minutes on each side.
Serve with a drizzle of soy dressing and the beet slices.

Warm Lionfish and Potato Salad
Serves 4

1½ lbs lionfish filets
4 limes—juice of
1 lb new potatoes
1 tbsp capers
10 anchovies, chopped
4 eggs
½ lb green beans
handful fresh chervil leaves
2 lemons—juice of
olive oil
seasoning

Slice the lionfish and marinade in the lime juice until cooked. Bring water to boil, add salt and new potatoes.

Place the new potatoes in salted boiling water and cook for 15 minutes. Drain, season and cut in half.

Place the green beans in boiling salted water and cook for 5 minutes, drain. Place the eggs in boiling water and cook for 8 minutes then refresh immediately in cold water, peel and quarter.

In a large bowl add the lemon juice and a good drizzle of olive oil, add the warm potatoes, warm beans, lionfish and all the other ingredients. Fold them together and serve.

Lionfish, Chorizo and Chickpea Stew

Serves 6

Invasive lionfish are out-living, out-eating, out-breeding and out-competing every other native fish in the Caribbean Sea, Western Atlantic Ocean and Gulf of Mexico and the Mediterranean. If left unchecked lionfish will ultimately cause the destruction of the native fish stocks, reefs and the livelihoods of everyone that depend upon them.

1 lb lionfish filets, roughly chopped
1 15 oz can chickpeas, washed
1 large onion diced
3 cans chopped tomatoes
1 pint chicken stock
1 lb chorizo, chopped
3 cloves garlic, finely chopped
7 oz roasted red peppers, skinned and sliced
1 tsp paprika
4 oz baby leaf spinach, washed

Sweat onion in a heavy based saucepan until soft, add chorizo and garlic and stir over the heat for 10 minutes.

Add all the other ingredients except the spinach and lionfish. Bring to boil and simmer for 10 minutes. Add the lionfish and spinach and simmer for an additional 3 minutes or until lionfish is cooked.

Lionfish, Black Bean and Mango Quesadillas

Makes 12 pieces

½ lb lionfish filets, slices
1 tbsp smoked paprika
4 flour tortillas
1 large mango, roughly chopped
1 tbsp vegetable oil
¼ lb grated cheddar
16 oz can black beans, drained and rinsed
4 tbsp pickled jalapenos
handful cilantro leaves
4 tbsp sour cream
4 tbsp salsa (page 73)

In a small bowl, toss the lionfish with the paprika and some salt and pepper. Heat a small frying pan with 1 tsp of the oil and sear the fish for 2 minutes, set to one side. Spread the cheese over 2 of the tortillas, sprinkle the black beans, mango, fish, jalapenos and cilantro leaves on top of the cheese, top with the other 2 tortillas. Divide the rest of the oil between 2 large frying pans and place the tortillas in the pans over a low-medium heat. Brown on one side for 3-4 minutes until the cheese is melted and the tortilla is golden, taking care not to let them burn. Turn over and cook for another 3 minutes. If the pan is looking a bit dry, add some more oil. Take them out and cut each into 6 pieces. Serve with sour cream, salsa and a sprinkle of cilantro and jalapenos.

Thai Style Fish Cakes
with Cucumber Salad and Sweet Chili Sauce

Serves 4

For the fish cakes
1 lb lionfish, cut into small pieces
½ red pepper, roughly chopped
2 red chilies, roughly chopped
2 tbsp cilantro leaves
3 spring onions, roughly chopped
2 cloves garlic, crushed
1 stalk lemongrass, tender part only, finely chopped
1 tbsp fish sauce
4 fl oz coconut milk
1 whole egg
4½ oz green beans, finely chopped
vegetable oil

For the cucumber salad
2 cucumbers, peeled, halved lengthwise and deseeded
1¼ oz caster sugar
2 fl oz rice wine vinegar
2 chilies, finely diced
1 tbsp nam pla (fish sauce)
2 tbsp chopped cilantro
1 tbsp chopped mint
1½ oz peanuts

Place the pepper, chilies, cilantro, spring onion, garlic, fish sauce and lemon grass into a food processor and blend to a paste. Add the fish pieces to the paste, blend well then mix to a smooth paste adding the egg and coconut milk. Place in a bowl, add the beans and refrigerate for at least 2 hours.

Cut the cucumber into ¼ inch slices. In a bowl dissolve the sugar in the vinegar add the cucumber and fold in the chilies and herbs. Half fill a heavy based pan with oil and heat over medium to high heat (do not leave unattended). Shape the paste into patties and carefully lower into the hot oil in batches (the oil should reach half way up the sides of the patties).

Fry until crisp and golden turning once during cooking, remove and place on paper towels to drain.

Add peanuts and fish sauce to the cucumber mix and serve with the fishcakes and sweet chili sauce (page 73).

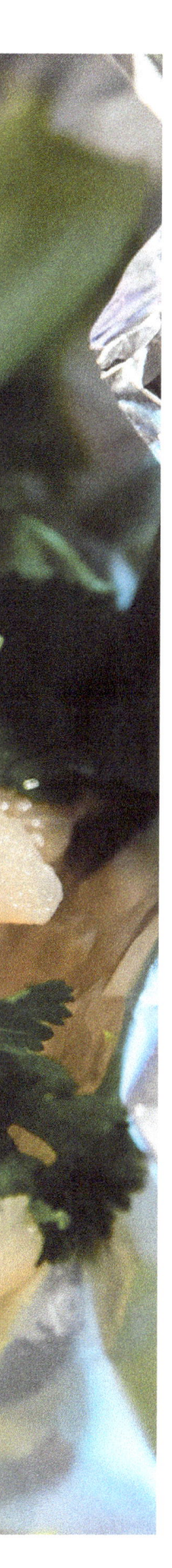

Entrees

Poached Lionfish and Tomato Risotto

Serves 6

34 fl oz fish stock
14 oz risotto rice
2 cloves garlic, crushed
1 small onion, sliced
2-3 tbsp of butter
2 wine glasses of dry white wine
1 pint cherry tomatoes, halved
2 lb lionfish
handful basil, torn
4 oz fresh parmesan, grated plus some shavings for serving

For poaching liquid
2 quarts coconut water
1 lb coconut flakes
1 onion, chopped
4 sprigs thyme, chopped
4 hot peppers of your choice, chopped
1 chili, chopped
4 fl oz rice white vinegar

For the poaching liquor
In a medium saucepan, sauté the onion until translucent and tender. Once the onion is soft, add the thyme, coconut flakes and peppers, cook until fragrant. Pour in the coconut water and vinegar. Bring the mixture to a boil and reduce to a gentle simmer for 10 minutes. Pour contents into a blender. Blend until smooth, then strain through a fine-mesh-strainer. Pour back into the pan.

Bring the poaching liquor to a simmer and add the lionfish filets, simmer for 2 minutes until tender, strain and set aside.
In a large heavy bottomed pan, sweat the onions and garlic in a little oil until translucent, add the rice and wine and bring to boil. As the rice absorbs the wine, slowly add the stock, reducing the heat to a simmer. Add the stock one ladle at a time letting the rice absorb the liquid each time until all the stock is added. This will take about 15 minutes.
Add the parmesan and place aside for a couple of minutes with the lid on. Stir in the lionfish, tomatoes and basil, season and serve.

Lionfish Pie

Serving size: 4 people

1 lb lionfish
2 lobster tails
1 lb shrimp
1 lb fresh spinach
½ cup white wine
salt and pepper to season
1 tbsp olive oil

Béchamel Sauce
2 cups of whole milk
1 tsp salt
6 tbsp of butter
3 tbsp of all-purpose flour
pinch of finely grated nutmeg

Cheese Rosti
4 large white potatoes
1 large onion
3 oz strong cheddar cheese (coarsely grated)
3 oz parmesan cheese (coarsely grated)

For the rosti, grate the potatoes on the course side of the grater. Set aside. Grate the onion on the course side of the grater. Put potatoes and onion into a colander and, using your hands, squeeze out as much of the excess liquid as you can. Season with salt and pepper and add the cheese.

Using 4 sheets of greased parchment paper, split the mix into quarters and flatten each quarter onto the paper. Sprinkle cheese onto each one and put to one side.

Preheat the oven to 350°F. Cut up the lobster into 1 inch pieces. Season the shrimp, lobster and lionfish with season all & salt and pepper. Place the lionfish, shrimp and lobster in an oven proof dish. Add the white wine and cover with foil and bake for 10 minutes. In a saucepan, heat olive oil and add spinach. Cook on a medium heat until the spinach has wilted.

Heat the butter until melted. Stir in the flour. Reduce the heat to low and stir until incorporated. Gradually stir in the milk. Bring to a boil, reduce the heat to medium and stir for 4-5 minutes or until sauce thickens. Season with salt and pepper and a pinch of finely grated nutmeg.

Preheat the oven to 400°F.

Break the lionfish into small chunks. Place the lionfish, lobster, shrimp and spinach into an oven proof dish. Spoon the béchamel sauce over the dish. Cover with foil and bake for 20 minutes.

Meanwhile, place the rostis under a hot broil/grill and grill until they turn golden brown. To serve, spoon fish mixture onto individual plates and place a cheese rosti on top.

Pan Fried Lionfish
with Caramelized Onions, Peas and Sweet Potato Fries served with Lemon & Cilantro Mayonnaise

Serves 4

For the onions
3 large onions, sliced
2 tsp spice mix
(I use a Belizean spice mix, but you can use any)
1 tbsp vegetable oil
3 handfuls frozen peas
few mint leaves, chopped

For the fish
2 lbs lionfish filets
plain flour, seasoned, to coat the fish
3 tbsp vegetable oil for frying

For the fries
2 large sweet potatoes, washed and cut into wedges
1 tsp smoked paprika
drizzle of olive oil

For the mayonnaise
3 tbsp mayonnaise (page 73)
1 lemon — juice of
handful cilantro, chopped

Preheat the oven to 400°F.
Add the lemon juice and cilantro to the mayonnaise and place in the refridgerator.
In a bowl, mix the sweet potatoes with seasoning, paprika and olive oil. Place in a large baking tray and roast in the oven for 30-40 minutes.
Meanwhile, coat the onions in the spice mix, place the oil in a large sauce pan and pan fry until soft, add peas and continue to stir until peas are just cooked, add chopped mint and season – set aside.
Place oil in large frying pan and preheat until hot but not smoking. Gently coat the fish filets with the seasoned flour and pan fry for 1-2 minutes on each side.
Serve the fish on top of the onion mixture with the fries and mayonnaise on the side.

If you never swim in the sea. If you do not eat seafood. If you have absolutely no interest in the oceans. This problem affects you!

50

Lionfish with Roasted New Potatoes, Chorizo, Pears and Parsley, Stilton and Walnut Pesto

Serves 4

2 lb lionfish filets
1 lb new potatoes
3 large pears, cored and sliced lengthwise
8 oz chorizo, diced and fried
handful parsley
1 clove garlic, crushed
handful walnut pieces, roasted
3 oz stilton (or any blue cheese)
lemon—juice of
2 fl oz olive oil

Preheat the oven to 350°F.
Place the new potatoes in a roasting pan, season with sea salt and black pepper. Drizzle with oil and bake for 10 minutes, add the pears and bake for another 10 minutes.
Place the parsley, walnuts, garlic, blue cheese, lemon juice and olive oil into a food processor and blend until smooth.
In a skillet, heat some oil to a medium heat and fry the seasoned fish for 1-2 minutes on each side, add the chorizo. Place the potatoes, pears, fish and chorizo on each plate and drizzle over the dressing to serve.

Lionfish with Bubble and Squeak, Poached Egg and Hollandaise

Serves 4
1½ lb lionfish filets

For the bubble and squeak
4 oz butter
1 onion, finely sliced
1 clove garlic, crushed
16 oz cold mashed potato
left over vegetables

For the hollandaise
1 stick melted butter
1 tbsp lemon juice
3 large egg yolks

For the poached eggs
seasoning
4 eggs
2 tsp white vinegar
1 tsp salt or to taste

Melt half the butter in a frying pan and sweat the onion and garlic until golden brown. In a large bowl mix the mashed potato, onion & garlic and the vegetables, season. Divide the mixture into 4 patties. Heat the rest of the butter in a frying pan and place the patties in the pan, frying them for 5 minutes on each side until golden brown and hot in the middle. Add some oil to the pan if necessary.

For the hollandaise, melt the butter in the microwave or in a pan, do not let it burn. Place the egg yolks and lemon juice in a food processor, blend for a couple of minutes then slowly add the melted butter, season.

Bring a pan of water to a boil and add the vinegar. Break the eggs into the boiling water, then turn down to a simmer (make sure there is enough water to cover the eggs and that the water is always moving). Simmer for 3-4 minutes then remove. Salt to taste.

Coat the lionfish with seasoned flour and pan-fry in hot oil for 3 minutes. Place the bubble and squeak on each plate, put the fish on top, place a poached egg on each fish and top with hollandaise.

Grilled Lionfish with Green Sauce, New Potatoes and Arugula

Serves 4

8 lionfish filets
2 cloves garlic
handful parsley
handful mint
handful chervil
10 salted anchovies
2 tsp capers
6 gherkin pickles
1 tbsp dijon mustard
8 tbsp olive oil
3 tbsp white wine vinegar
black pepper
1½ lbs new potatoes
3.5 oz arugula

Mix the mustard, vinegar and olive oil in a bowl. Finely chop the garlic, anchovies, gherkin pickles and all of the fresh herbs. Place in the bowl and add the capers.
Place the new potatoes in a pan of salted boiling water and cook for 15 minutes, drain and add sea salt.
Grill the lionfish under a hot grill for 4 minutes, serve with the green sauce on top of the fish with the new potatoes and arugula.

Lionfish Mexican Chili

1 large onion diced
2 cloves garlic, crushed
handful fresh cilantro leaves
1 lb lionfish filets, sliced
1 tbsp olive oil
1 tsp ground cumin
½ tsp ground cilantro
2 red chilies, finely chopped
1 15 oz can chopped tomatoes
1 15 oz can black beans, drained and rinsed
4-6 flour tortillas
shredded lettuce
4 tbsp Greek yogurt
lime wedges

In a large pan sweat onion until soft. Add the chili, garlic, fish and spices, cook for 5 minutes, stirring occasionally. Add the tomatoes and beans. Bring to boil and simmer for 5 minutes. Add fresh cilantro and season.

Serve on flour tortillas with shredded lettuce, yogurt and lime wedges.

Lionfish Couscous
with Chili Mint Yogurt
Serve 4

8 lionfish filets
2 medium zucchinis, halved lengthwise and cut into half moons
1 red onion, sliced thinly
7oz cherry tomatoes, halved
2 red chilies, finely chopped
small handful fresh cilantro leaves
10 oz couscous
7 fl oz chili sauce (page 73)
6 tbsp natural yogurt
small handful fresh mint leaves
1 tsp honey

In a bowl mix the yogurt with 1 chili, the finely chopped mint leaves and honey.

Place the couscous in a bowl. Season. Cover with 10 oz (so that it's just covering the couscous) of boiling water. Cover with plastic wrap film and set aside.

In a pan fry the onion and chili until the onion is soft. Add the zucchini and lionfish and fry until they start to color. Add the cherry tomatoes and stir for 1 minute. Take off the plastic wrap and fluff up the couscous with a fork. Add the vegetable and fish mixture. Stir in the cilantro and serve with the chili mint yogurt.

Southern Asian Spiced Lionfish
with Coconut Rice
Serves 4

8 lionfish filets
pinch sea salt
1 red chili, finely chopped
1 clove garlic, crushed
3 tbsp vegetable oil
2 oz butter

For the Sauce
4 tbsp vegetable oil
1 inch ginger, finely chopped
1 red chili, finely chopped
1 clove garlic, crushed
1 green chili, finely chopped
3 shallots finely chopped
1 tsp turmeric
1 tsp cayenne pepper
14 oz fish stock
4 tbsp double cream
4 oz butter

For the Rice
12 oz basmati rice
7 oz coconut milk
juice 3 limes
handful cilantro

Rub the lionfish with the red chili, garlic and sea salt, set aside. In a heavy based sauce pan, fry the ginger, garlic, shallots and chilies until the shallots are soft. Add the stock, turmeric and cayenne. Bring to a boil and reduce to half. Add the double cream and butter.
Place the rice in a pan with the coconut milk and lime juice. Add water until the rice is just covered. Bring to a boil. Simmer for 5 minutes then leave with a lid on for 15 minutes.
Pan fry the fish in hot oil for 3 minutes, add butter to the pan and spoon over the fish.
Serve the fish on the sauce with the rice on the side, sprinkle with fresh cilantro.

Lionfish
with Sweet Potato Fries, Brussel Sprout Puree, Parmesan Baked Fennel and Lemon Butter
Serves 4

8 lionfish filets
vegetable oil
3 oz butter
1 lemon
½ lb brussels sprouts, trimmed
¼ cup heavy cream
1 tbsp butter
handful mint leaves
seasoning
2 fennel bulbs, trimmed and split lengthwise
½ cup parmesan grated
2 large sweet potatoes cut into strips
olive oil

Preheat the oven to 400°F.
Place the sweet potatoes onto an oven tray, sprinkle with oil, season and place in the oven for 20 minutes or until golden. In a separate tray place the fennel bulbs, sprinkle with oil and bake for 15 minutes. Sprinkle with the parmesan and bake for an additional 5 minutes. Meanwhile place the brussels sprouts in salted boiling water and boil for 6 minutes until tender but still bright green. Strain and place in a food processor with the butter, cream, mint and seasoning. Blend until smooth. Place the seasoned fish in a medium skillet and fry for 1-2 minutes on each side. Place the butter in the pan. Baste and squeeze the lemon juice over the fish.
Serve the fish with the fries, fennel and puree. Spoon the butter and lemon over the fish.

Parmesan and Herb Crusted Lionfish
with Warm Asparagus, Tenderstem Broccoli and Zucchini Salad

Serves 2

2 lb lionfish filets
2 tbsp parsley, finely chopped
4 tbsp parmesan, finely grated
4 tbsp breadcrumbs
1 zucchini, cut into half moons
4 oz asparagus tips
6 oz tenderstem broccoli, trimmed
4 oz baby spinach leaves
handful chervil leaves
handful parsley leaves
olive oil
1 lemon — juice of

Season the zucchini, drizzle with oil and place in a preheated oven at 400°F for 10 minutes. Meanwhile put a salted pan of water on the stove to boil. Mix the parmesan, breadcrumbs and parsley in a bowl and spread over one side of each fish filet.

Place in the oven and bake for 7 minutes. Place the broccoli and asparagus into the boiling water and boil for 3 minutes, drain. In a bowl mix the vegatables with the spinach until the spinach starts to wilt a little, add the herbs, olive oil and lemon juice, Divide between 2 bowls and serve with the baked fish on top.

Lionfish Goujons
with Oven Roasted Chips and Tartare Sauce

Serves 4

8 lionfish filets cut into strips
3 oz plain flour
2 eggs
6 oz breadcrumbs
4 tbsp mayonnaise (page 73)
6 oz capers
6 oz cornichons (gherkin pickles), chopped
small handful fresh parsley, chopped
small handful fresh dill, chopped
1 lemon — juice of
seasoning
1½ lb baking potatoes
olive oil
sea salt
black pepper
handful fresh rosemary

To make the tartare sauce, add the capers, cornichons, dill, parsley and lemon juice to the mayonnaise and set aside.
Coat the fish in the flour, dip in beaten egg then coat in breadcrumbs.
Slice the potatoes into chunks, place in an oven tray and sprinkle with oil, sea salt and the rosemary sprigs. Place in the oven and bake at 400°F for 45 minutes, stiring occasionally.
In a deep fat fryer or heavy based saucepan heat the oil to 375°F or until the breadcrumbs sizzle.
Place the fish in the deep fat fryer and fry for 2 minutes until golden.

Lionfish and Shrimp Fish Cakes
with Mango Salsa
Serves 4

For the Fish Cakes
10 oz lionfish, cooked
7 oz shrimp, peeled, de-veined and cooked
2 medium potatoes, cooked and mashed
1 cup breadcrumbs
1 handful fresh parsley
2 tbsp fresh parmesan, grated
1 med carrot, grated
1 small can sweet corn, drained
2 eggs, beaten
flour for dusting
seasoning

For the Salsa
1 large mango, diced
1 red chili, finely chopped
1 small red onion, finely diced
1 large avocado, diced
handful cilantro, chopped
2 limes—juice of

For the salsa, mix all the ingredients together in a bowl and set aside.
For the fish cakes add all the ingredients, mix well. If the mixture is too dry add more egg, if it's too wet add more breadcrumbs.
Make into patties, dust with flour and fry in a frying pan in hot oil until golden brown on each side. Serve with fries.

Pan fried Lionfish & New Potatoes
Roasted Sweet Pepper, Fennel with Chili Mint Dressing and Pea Puree

Serves 4

2 lb lionfish filets
1 lb new potatoes
2 red peppers, sliced
1 large fennel bulb, sliced
1 red chili, finely chopped
14 oz frozen peas
2-3 tbsp butter
splash double cream
tbsp fresh mint leaves, finely chopped
1 small garlic clove, crushed
6 oz vegetable oil

Preheat the oven to 400°F. Place the potatoes in a roasting pan with sea salt and vegetable oil and roast for 30 minutes. Place the vegetables in a separate roasting tin. Drizzle with oil and seasoning and roast for 20 minutes.
Place the chili, half the mint, garlic and oil in a bowl and whisk together.
Place the peas in a pan of boiling salted water and cook for 3 minutes. Drain then place in a food processor with the butter, rest of the mint and cream. Season and blend.
Dust the fish with seasoned flour then fry the lionfish for 1-2 minutes on each side.
Arrange the potatoes on each plate, top with the roasted vegetables. Add the puree. Place the fish on top then drizzle the dressing over each one.

Lionfish, Tomato and Spinach Pancakes

Serves 4

plain flour
eggs
milk
seasoning
6 oz fresh spinach
4 cups chopped tomatoes
1 lb lionfish filets, roughly chopped
1 onion, chopped
2 garlic cloves, crushed
½ cup crème fraiche
small handful fresh parsley, chopped
small handful fresh chervil, chopped
2 large handfuls of grated cheddar

Preheat oven to 350°F.
Take a 16 oz glass and fill with flour then pour into a bowl, then fill the glass with eggs, pour onto the flour and repeat with the milk so that equal volumes are used. Use an immersion blender to make a batter. Let it sit for 15 minutes. In a non-stick pan heat a little oil until hot. Ladle the batter into the pan and swirl so that the pan is covered. Cook for 1-2 minutes on each side, set aside and repeat the process until you have made either 4 large or 8 small pancakes.
In a pan sweat the onion until soft. Add the garlic and lionfish and cook for 2 minutes. Add the tomatoes and bring to a boil. Take off the heat and add the spinach letting it wilt in the mixture. Add the crème fraiche, fresh herbs and season.
In an oven tray place a pancake and fill lengthwise with the fish mixture, fold over and repeat with the other pancakes. Sprinkle with cheese and bake for 15 minutes or until the cheese is golden.

Blackened Lionfish Burritos

Serves 6

- 1 tbsp paprika
- 2 tsps dry mustard
- 1 tsp cayenne pepper
- 1 tsp ground cumin
- 1 tsp black pepper
- 1 tsp white pepper
- 1 tsp salt
- ¾ cup unsalted butter, melted
- 1 lb lionfish filets
- ¼ cup unsalted butter, melted

In a small bowl, mix together paprika, dry mustard, cayenne pepper, cumin, black pepper, white pepper, thyme and salt. Set aside.

Heat a heavy cast iron pan or a comal on high heat until extremely hot, about 10 minutes.

Pour ¾ cup melted butter into a shallow dish. Dip each fillet into butter, turning once to coat both sides. Sprinkle both sides of filets with spice mixture, and gently pat mixture onto fish.

Place filets into hot pan or comal without crowding. Carefully pour about 1 tsp melted butter over each fillet. Cook until fish has a charred appearance, about ½ a minute. Turn filets, spoon 1 tsp melted butter over each, and cook until charred. Repeat with remaining fish.

Serve with mayonnaise in a flour tortilla with a salad mix of your choice.

BBQ Curried Lionfish

1 tsp soy sauce
1 tsp curry powder
1 tbsp olive oil
1 garlic clove
1 tsp cumin
1 tsp sesame oil
1 tsp finely grated fresh ginger
1 lb lionfish filet
½ lb baby tomatoes
pinch of salt
½ small onion – sliced
few sprigs of cilantro
foil
1 lime

In a small bowl, whisk olive oil with soy, curry powder, garlic, ginger, cumin and sesame oil. Place lionfish in a large resealable bag and pour in soy mixture. Squeeze as much air as possible from bag. Seal tightly with an elastic band as close to fish as possible. Massage to evenly coat with marinade. Leave at room temperature for 15 minutes.

Meanwhile, oil grill and heat barbecue to medium-high. Place banana leaves on foil.

Remove filets from marinade. Evenly spread lionfish onto the banana leaves, add sliced onion and sliced baby tomatoes and a pinch of salt. Wrap the banana leaves and cover with the foil.

Place on BBQ and barbecue for 5 mins on each side or until lionfish is cooked. Serve with slice of lime and a couple of sprigs of cilantro.

Lionfish with Chips and Mushy Peas

Serve 4

For the Fish
2 lb lionfish, filets
2 quarts vegetable or sunflower oil for frying
1 cup plain flour
2 tbsp garlic powder
2 tbsp paprika
1 tsp salt
2 tsp pepper
2 eggs beaten
1 can beer

For the Mushy Peas
1 lb frozen peas
2 tbsp butter
1 lemon—juice of
1 tbsp fresh mint, chopped
dash heavy cream

For the chips
2 lb Maris Piper potatoes
sunflower oil
sea salt

Rinse fish, pat dry and season. Combine garlic powder, flour, paprika and seasoning. Stir in egg and gradually whisk in the beer until a batter is formed. Let it sit for up to 3 hours.

Chop the potatoes into finger size chips, leaving the skin on. In a deep fat fryer heat the oil to 280°F, lower the chips in and blanch for around 8 minutes until soft but not colored.

In a pan stir the peas and butter until the peas are cooked but still a bright green, add the lemon, mint and cream and place the mixture in a food processor. Blend until they are mushy, season.

Turn the heat of the deep fat fryer to 350°F and fry the chips in 2 batches until they are golden brown. Drain on paper towels. Sprinkle with sea salt.

Turn the heat up to 365°F, dip the fish in the batter and drop them, 2 at a time into the hot oil, turning once until both sides are golden. Drain on paper towels.

Serve with lemon wedges.

Thai Style Baked Lionfish

Serves 4

8 lionfish filets
1 inch root ginger, chopped
2 cloves garlic, chopped
2 red chilies, sliced, finely
2 limes, juice and zest
6 baby bok choy, each quartered lengthwise
4 tbsp soy sauce
handful cilantro leaves

Nestle the seasoned fish side by side on large squares of foil. Scatter ginger, garlic, chili and lime zest over the fish, drizzle the lime juice on top and scatter the bok choy and cilantro on top and around the fish. Pour on soy sauce and loosely seal the foil leaving space on top for the steam to escape. Place on grease proof tray and bake in oven at 400°F for 10 minutes. Serve with coconut rice.

Caribbean Lionfish Curry

Serves 4

1 onion, diced
3 cloves garlic, crushed
2 red bell peppers, chopped
1 tomato, chopped
½ tsp dried chilies
1 tsp curry powder
1 tsp cumin
1 15 oz can chopped tomatoes
1 can coconut milk
1½ lb lionfish filets
seasoning
lime—juice of
cilantro leaves

Sweat the onion in a large pan until soft, add the garlic, peppers, tomato and spices. Stir over the heat for a few minutes then add the chopped tomatoes, bringing to a boil. Simmer for 5 minutes then add the coconut milk.

In a separate frying pan, fry the fish filets in hot oil for 1-2 minutes each side. To serve, place the curry in each bowl, divide the lionfish filets between each bowl, squeeze lime juice over each one and sprinkle some cilantro leaves over. Serve with coconut rice.

Crispy Fried Lionfish Noodles

1 lb lionfish filets cut into strips
4 tbsp corn flour
3 tsp chinese 5 spice powder
6 oz vegetable oil
2 red peppers, finely diced
2 red chilies, finely sliced
5 spring onions, sliced, green and white parts separated
3 cloves garlic, crushed
thumb size ginger, finely sliced
5 tbsp rice wine vinegar
2 tbsp soy sauce
3 tbsp sweet chili sauce
3 tbsp tomato ketchup
8 oz fresh egg noodles

Place the fish in a bowl and toss in the corn flour and 5 spice powder. Heat the oil in a wok until hot then add the fish and fry until golden and crisp, scoop out and drain on paper towels. Pour away all but 1 tbsp of the oil and add the pepper, ½ chili, the white ends of the spring onion, garlic and ginger and fry for 3 minutes. In a jug, mix the vinegar, soy sauce, chili sauce and ketchup with 3 tbsp of water. Pour the mixture into the pan, boil for 2 minutes then add the fish, toss well. Place the noodles in a pan of boiling water and cook for 1 minute, drain. Serve the fish mixture with the noodles, sprinkle the green ends of the onion and the rest of the chili on top.

Fish unlike mammals do not pass on education to the next generation. Therefore, it is not seen as a solution to feed other species to encourage natural predation. In places where divers have fed lionfish to sharks, moray eels, groupers and barracudas. These species have rarely fed on lionfish by themselves. And in some places, predators are recognizing the divers as the food source and not the lionfish, leading to diver attacks! When divers feed lionfish to other species, there is no means of creating vertical markets such as lionfish on menus or as jewelry because the other species will grab the lionfish off the spear as soon as the diver has speared it!

There are some instances where groupers have hunted and eaten lionfish, however a recent study shows that native species are having almost no effect on the total lionfish population.

Here is what we do know today – these facts are proven:

Native fish stocks are down as a direct and identifiable result of lionfish predation.
Commercial fisheries and the lobster industry in places like Florida & the Caribbean are crashing as a direct result of lionfish predation.
Reef health in the Western Atlantic Basin is in serious decline.
The lionfish population continues to grow at an ALARMING rate and they are establishing their range further south into South America every day.
The areas that are regularly maintained by lionfish hunters are seeing a demonstrable rebound of native fish and other sea creatures.

We are rapidly running out of time as we are approaching a tipping point from which our underwater ecosystems cannot recover. Direct action by lionfish hunters is a viable method for controlling lionfish populations in the very, very small area that we can reach, relative to the entire range of the new lionfish habitat. Trap research is showing promising results for deeper control.

Coconut, Lime & Cilantro Lionfish

Serves 2

1 lb lionfish filets
½ can coconut milk
½ onion
½ lime
lime zest from one lime
1 handful of chopped cilantro
1 tbsp vegetable oil
1 tbsp olive oil
5 cloves garlic
seasoning

Season lionfish with all purpose seasoning, salt and black pepper.
Heat vegetable oil and fast fry lionfish filets on a hot heat for 2 minutes.
Remove filets.
Clean frying pan and soften onions in hot olive oil.
Add chopped garlic and stir for 1 minute.
Add lime zest.
Add coconut milk.
Season with salt & pepper.
Simmer for 5 minutes.
Add lime juice.
Add cooked lionfish and heat through.

Sprinkle with cilantro and serve.

Lionfish Tempura
with Sesame Broccoli and Cauliflower

Serves 4

2 lb lionfish filets
3 oz plain flour
1 tbsp corn flour
pinch Chinese five spice power
½ tsp sea salt
sunflower oil for frying
7 fl oz sparkling mineral water
1 lb broccoli and cauliflower florets
1 tbsp sesame oil
2 tbsp sesame seeds, toasted
1 tbsp soy sauce
1 red chili, sliced

Sieve the flour, corn flour, salt and spice into a bowl, whisk in the mineral water along with a few ice cubes. Don't over beat it (it doesn't matter about a few lumps).

Heat the oil in a large wok, a third full, to 375°F. Dip some of the fish into the batter, shake off any excess then lower straight into the hot oil (don't crowd the pan) until crisp, drain on paper towels.

Prepare the broccoli and cauliflower by steaming for 4 minutes. Heat the sesame oil in a wok over a high heat, add the vegetables, sesame seeds, remove from the heat, add the soy sauce and sprinkle on sliced chili.

Lionfish with Tarka Dal and Cilantro Salad

Serves 4

2 lb lionfish filets
2-3 tbsp butter
2 tbsp vegetable oil

For the Tarka Dal
9 oz chana dal (yellow lentils)
3 tbsp cumin seeds
1 small onion, chopped
¾ inch ginger, peeled and sliced
3 garlic cloves
3 tomatoes
¾ tsp tumeric
¾ tsp ground masala
handful chopped cilantro
5 oz cherry tomatoes, quartered
seasoning

For the Salad
1 red onion, thinly sliced
¼ cucumber, deseeded and sliced
olive oil
lemon juice
bunch cilantro leaves

Place the lentils and 1¾ pints of the water into a pan, stir well and bring to a boil. Skim off any froth that forms on the surface of the water with a spoon. Cover the pan with a lid and reduce the heat to a simmer. Simmer, stirring regularly, for 35-40 minutes, or until the lentils are just tender, adding more water as necessary. When the lentils have cooked through, remove the pan from the heat and use a whisk to break down the lentils. Set the mixture aside to thicken and cool. Meanwhile, heat the oil in a pan over a medium heat. Add the cumin seeds and fry for 20-30 seconds, or until fragrant. Add the onion, chilies and ginger and fry for 4-5 minutes, or until golden-brown. Blend the garlic and tomatoes to a purée in a food processor. Add the purée to the pan and stir well to combine. Add the ground spices and 3½ fl oz of water to the pan and stir well to combine. Season, to taste, with salt and simmer over a medium heat for 15-20 minutes, or until the oil from the sauce has risen to the surface of the sauce. Add the cooked lentils to the sauce and stir well, adding more water as necessary to loosen the mixture. Bring the mixture to a boil and season, to taste, with salt and freshly ground black pepper. Stir in the chopped cilantro and cherry tomatoes just before serving. In a bowl toss together the onion, cucumber a good splash of olive oil, lemon juice and cilantro leaves.
Put the oil in a non-stick skillet and place over a medium heat, cook the seasoned fish for 1-2 minutes on each side add 2-3 tbsp of butter to the pan, baste the fish and remove from the pan.
Serve the fish with the dal and the salad on the side.

Seared Lionfish
on a Spiced Sweet Potato Mash with Soy Sauce and Ginger Dressing

Serves 4

2 lb lionfish filets
flour for dusting
3 tbsp vegetable oil
sea salt and black pepper

For the Mash
1 lb orange-fleshed sweet potatoes, peeled and diced
1 small onion, chopped
1 tsp ground cumin
1 tsp ground cilantro
2 tsp grated ginger
1 chili, finely chopped
2 cloves garlic, crushed
8 fl oz coconut milk
handful fresh cilantro

For the Dressing
2 tsp grated ginger
4 spring onions, finely sliced
5 fl oz light soy sauce
1 tbsp vegetable oil
1 tsp honey

For the mash, heat the oil in a heavy based pan, add the sweet potatoes, onion, cumin and cilantro, sweat for 5 minutes until soft but not brown. Stir in the ginger, garlic, chili and coconut milk, season lightly with a pinch of salt and bring to a boil. Cover the pan and simmer over a low heat for 15 minutes until the potatoes are cooked. Drain the potatoes. Mash the mixture well and keep warm.

For the sauce mix all the ingredients together. Heat the oil in a frying pan until nearly smoking, dust the fish with the seasoned flour and sear in oil for 1-2 minutes on each side. Stir the cilantro into the mash and serve the fish on the mash and drizzle over the dressing. Serve with wilted spinach.

Extra Bits

Mayonnaise
4 egg yolks
1/2 lemon — juice of
1 pint vegetable oil
salt and pepper

Place the yolks and lemon juice in a food processor, blend until the yolks start to pale then slowly add the oil until it thickens. Add seasoning.

Cajun Seasoning
6 tbsp smoked paprika
4 tsps salt
4 tsps dried minced garlic, such as schwartz
4 tsps crushed chilies
2 tsps coarsely ground black pepper
2 tsps dried oregano
2 tsps ground cilantro

Sweet Chili Sauce
½ cup soy sauce
2 tbsp rice vinegar
1 tbsp Asian style chili paste
1 tbsp honey
1 tbsp grated ginger
1 tbsp toasted sesame seeds

Combine all ingredients in a bowl and stir.

Tomato Salsa
red chili, finely chopped
4 ripe tomatoes, finely diced
½ bunch fresh cilantro leaves, finely chopped
2 limes — juice of
½ small red onion, finely diced

Mix all the ingredients together in a bowl.

Pesto Dressing
2 cloves garlic, crushed
handful parmesan, grated
bunch basil
8 tbsp olive oil

Place all ingredients in a food processor and blend.

Chipotle
4 garlic cloves
2 dried chipotle chilies
2 dried Ancho chilies
1 ½ tsp dried oregano
½ lime

Preheat oven to 350°F

Place the unpeeled garlic cloves in a roasting tin and place in the oven for 15-20 minutes or until soft, transfer to a plate, allow to cool and remove the skins. Place the chilies in a bowl, pour over boiling water to just cover and leave for 15 minutes. Drain, reserving the liquid and place the chilies with the garlic and oregano in a blender with a large pinch of salt, blend to a paste. Add the juice of the lime and 4 tbsp of the reserved liquid and blend to combine.

Tabbouleh
2 oz bulgur wheat
2 oz flat parsley, chopped
2 oz mint, chopped
7 oz ripe tomatoes, deseeded and chopped
3 spring onions, finely diced
1 lemon — juice of
3 tbsp olive oil

Place the bulgur wheat in a bowl. Pour 7fl oz of boiling water over the bulgur wheat. Cover with plastic wrap and leave for 30 minutes.
Place the herbs into a bowl, add the tomatoes and spring onions. Thoroughly drain the bulgur wheat and add to the herb mix along with the lemon juice and olive oil, mix, season and serve.

Soy Sauce and Ginger Dressing
2 tsp grated ginger
4 spring onions, finely sliced
5 fl oz light soy sauce
1 tbsp vegetable oil
1 tsp honey

Place all ingredients in a bowl and whisk together.

Hot Sauce
1 onion, slices
3 garlic cloves, crushed
7 oz chilies
2 lb chopped tomatoes
5 oz dried dates
large handful cilantro
small handful mint

In a pan sweat the onion until soft, add the chilies and garlic and continue to fry for 5-10 minutes. Add the tomatoes and dates, bring to a boil and simmer for 20 minutes. Add the fresh herbs and blend.

Guest Recipes
Lionfish Potato Mousse

12 ounces lionfish
4 oz butter
10 oz potato (roughly one large russet or similar potato)
½ cup heavy cream
2 tbsp chopped chives
2 tbsp chopped cilantro
2 tsp kosher salt
black pepper to taste

Peel potato, cut into medium chunks and boil in salted water until soft. Drain, reserving potato.

Meanwhile, melt butter in small pot. Add lionfish and cook covered over low heat until lionfish is cooked through.

Place drained potato, lionfish with the butter, heavy cream, salt and pepper in food processor and process until smooth.

Add chopped cilantro and chives and pulse to blend.

Adjust seasoning to taste.

Serve slightly warm or at room temperature with sweet potato chips or crackers.

Spicy Lionfish & Snapper Ceviche, Avocado Purée on Tostones

4 filets of lionfish, diced
1 filet of snapper, diced (same size as lionfish)
4 limes juiced
1 habanero pepper
½ cup pineapple
salt & pepper

¼ cup carrot, small diced
¼ cup tomato, small diced
¼ cup cucumber, small diced
¼ cup red onion, small diced
1 jalepeño pepper, seeded & small diced

3 tbsp chopped chives
3 tbsp chopped cilantro

For the Ceviche:
Add habanero, lime juice and pineapple to the jar of a blender and blend on high for 30 seconds.
Season fish lightly with salt and pepper. Strain juice mixture over fish, careful not to press the solids (unless you want it REALLY spicy). Mix fish and lime juice together and let marinate until fish changes color slightly. Add vegetables to the fish and stir. Let marinate for 10 minutes.
Mix in chives and cilantro right before serving.

For Tostones:
3 plantains, green.
Vegetable oil, enough to fill a deep pot at least 3 inches, heated to 350 degrees.
Cut ends off plantains, peel.
Cut into 1-1.5 inch pieces. Fry in batches until they float. Remove from oil and flatten with the backside of a plate or bottom of a coffee mug. Fry the flattened pieces until crisp and golden on the edges. Remove from oil with a slotted spoon and sprinkle with a little salt. Set aside.

For Avocado Purée
4 ripe avocados
1 lime juiced
salt & pepper
1 small bunch cilantro leaves
3 tbsp chives
Place ingredients in a food processor and blend until smooth. Taste and add more salt or lime juice if needed.

For Garnish:
2 bunches chives or scallions
Oiled and season with salt & pepper
Grill until slightly charred, but not burnt
1 lime, cut in half and sliced thin
1 jalepeño, sliced thin in rounds

To assemble:
Arrange tostones on a plate, top with a spoon of avocado puree, scatter charred scallions. Squeeze out a bit of liquid from ceviche and put on top puree. Garnish with lime & jalepeño slices.

Acknowledgments

Jim Clarkson for his fabulous design and his endless patience with us.

James Travis, Saskia Van-Manen, Shiv Martin, Emma Hanlon and Paloma Ivanova for helping to create and style the recipe photos.

Belcampo Lodge, Maya Beach Bistro for allowing us to use their recipes.

Susan Genussa for proofreading.

Lionfish University, Reef Savers, Reef Conservation International, Blue Reef Adventures, 11th Hour Racing and all the other organizations that are helping to combat the lionfish invasion.

Our lovely customers at Souper Juice for valuable feedback and advice.

To all our friends and family for supporting us through this project.

Claire Wood and Polly Alford are hereby identified as the authors of this work in accordance with section 77 of the Copyright Designs Patients Act 1988 in collaboration with Lionfish University, a 501c3 non-profit. All rights reserved. No reproduction copy or transmission of this publication may be made without written permission. No paragraph of this publication may be reproduced, copied or transmitted save with written permission as in accordance with the Provisions of the Copyright Act 1956 (as amended). Any persons who does any unauthorised act in relation to this publication may be liable to criminal prosecution and civil claims for damages.

Index

A

Alford, Polly 1, 76
Anchovies 41, 53
Appetizers 15–33
Monica Archer 6
Arugula 12, 53
   Grilled Lionfish with Green Sauce, New Potatoes and Arugula 53
Asparagus 58
   Parmesan and Herb crusted Lionfish with warm Asparagus, Tenderstem Broccoli and Zucchini Salad 58
Avocado 16, 25, 26, 60, 75

B

Bacon 23
BBQ curried Lionfish 64
Beans 22, 31, 41, 43, 44, 54
   Black Beans 43, 54
Beer 19, 29, 65
Beets 32, 40
   Lionfish, Beetroot, New Potato and Lambs Lettuce Salad with Horseradish Crème Fraiche 32
   Lionfish with Pickled Beets and Ginger Cabbage 40
Black Beans 43, 54
Blackened Lionfish Burritos 63
Blue Reef Adventures 4, 76
Bok Choy 66
Broccoli 58, 70
Brunch 9–13
Brussels Sprouts 57
Burgers 38
   Spiced Lionfish Burgers 38
Burritos 63
   Blackened Lionfish Burritos 63
Butternut Squash 6, 17
   Butternut Squash and Green Chili Soup with Lionfish Ceviche 17

C

Cabbage 28, 37, 40
Cajun Seasoning 38, 73
Capers 41, 53, 59
Caribbean Lionfish Curry 67
Carrots 31
Cauliflower 70
Ceviche 17, 33, 75
   Butternut Squash and Green Chili Soup with Lionfish Ceviche 17
   Spicy Lionfish & Snapper Ceviche, Avocado Purée on Tostones 75
Cheese 6, 12, 30, 49
   Cheddar Cheese 49
   Cream Cheese 30
   Parmesan 6, 49, 57, 58, 60, 73
   Ricotta 12
Cherry Tomatoes 6, 25, 48, 55, 71
Chickpeas 24, 42
Chili 11, 16, 17, 18, 19, 28, 31, 33, 44, 48, 54, 55, 56, 60, 61, 66, 68, 70, 72, 73
Chilies 22, 31, 33, 44, 54, 55, 66, 67, 68, 73
Chipotle 25, 73
Chorizo 42, 51
Chowder 23
   Smoked Haddock, Lionfish, Spinach & Bacon Chowder 23
Cilantro 11, 16, 18, 20, 26, 28, 31, 33, 37, 38, 43, 44, 50, 54, 55, 56, 60, 64, 66, 67, 69, 71, 72, 73, 74
Clarkson, Jim 5, 76
Coconut, lime & cilantro Lionfish 69
Coconut milk 17, 21, 31, 44, 56, 67, 69, 72
Corn 22, 32, 37, 60
Cornichons 53, 59
Couscous 55
Cream Cheese 30
Crispy Fried Lionfish Noodles 68
Croquettes 24
   Lionfish and Wasabi Croquettes 24
Cucumber 25, 36, 44, 71
Curried 64
Curry 64, 67

E

Egg 10, 28, 44, 52, 68, 73
   Lionfish Frittatas with Tabbouleh 12
   Lionfish, Quinoa and Chili Omelette with Cilantro 11
   Lionfish Eggs Benedict 10
   Lionfish with Bubble and Squeak, Poached Egg and Hollandaise 52
Entrees 47–75

F

Fava Beans 22
Fennel 57, 61
Fish Cakes 44, 60
Fish Sauce 18
Fish stock 48
Frank, Stacy 5
Frittatas, Lionfish Frittatas with Tabbouleh 12
Frittatas 12

G

Genussa, Susan 76
Green Beans 31, 41, 44
Green Chilies 17
Grilled Lionfish with Green Sauce, New Potatoes and Arugula 53
Groupers 68

H

Hart, Jim 5
Hollandaise 10, 52
Hot Sauce 16, 73
Hudut-traditional Garifuna meal 21

L

Lime 16, 18, 20, 25, 26, 33, 37, 54, 64, 67, 69, 73
Lime Marinated Lionfish Salad 20
Lime marinated Lionfish Salad with Tomatoes, Avocado, Cucumber and Chipotle 25
Lionfish à la Monica 6
Lionfish and Shrimp Fish Cakes with Mango Salsa 60
Lionfish and Wasabi Croquettes 24
Lionfish, Beetroot, New Potato and Lambs Lettuce Salad with Horseradish Crème Fraiche 32
Lionfish, Black Bean and Mango Quesadillas 43
Lionfish, Chorizo and Chickpea Stew 42
Lionfish Cous Cous with Chili Mint Yogurt 55
Lionfish Goujons with Oven Roasted Chips and Tartare Sauce 59
Lionfish Mexican Chili 54
Lionfish Pate 30
Lionfish pie 49
Lionfish Potato Mousse 74
Lionfish salad with lychee and Chili 18
Lionfish Spring Rolls with Mango Salad and Hot Sauce 16
Lionfish Straws 19
Lionfish tacos 37
Lionfish Tempura with Sesame Broccoli and Cauliflower 70
Lionfish, Tomato and Spinach Pancakes 62
Lionfish University 1, 5, 6, 76
Lionfish with Bubble and Squeak, Poached Egg and Hollandaise 52
Lionfish with Chips and Mushy Peas 65
Lionfish with Ginger, Chili and Spring Onion 33
Lionfish with Pickled Beets and Ginger Cabbage 40
Lionfish with Roasted New Potatoes, Chorizo, Pears and Parsley, Stilton and Walnut Pesto 51
Lionfish with Sweet Potato Fries, Brussel Sprout Puree, Parmesan Baked Fennel and Lemon Butter 57
Lionfish with Sweet Potato Toast, Avocado and Cilantro & Lime Crème Fraiche 26
Lionfish with Tarka Dal and Cilantro Salad 71
Lionfish Wontons with Sweet Chili and Soy Sauce 28
Lionfish wrapped in Parma Ham stuffed with Mozzarella on Pesto Toast 27
Lobster 13, 49, 68
Lychees 18

M

Mango 16, 20, 43, 60
Mayonnaise 36, 50, 59, 73
Mersea Marine Conservation Consulting 2
Mesoamerican Reef 32
Mint 12, 22, 29, 37, 44, 50, 53, 55, 57, 61, 65, 73
Mushrooms 31

O

Onions 21, 23, 28, 33, 48, 50, 69, 73

P

Pancakes 62
  Lionfish, Tomato and Spinach Pancakes 62
Pan fried Lionfish & New Potatoes Roasted Sweet Pepper, Fennel with Chili Mint Dressing and Pea Puree 61
Pan-fried Lionfish Sandwich with Pickled Cucumber and Lemon Mayonnaise 36
Pan fried Lionfish with Caramelized Onions, Peas and Sweet Potato Fries served with Lemon & Cilantro Mayonnaise 50
Parmesan 6, 49, 57, 58, 60, 73
Parmesan and Herb crusted Lionfish with warm Asparagus, Tenderstem Broccoli and Zucchini Salad 58
Pate 30
  Lionfish Pate 30
Pea and Mint Soup with Crispy Lionfish 29
Peas 13, 29, 50, 61, 65
Peppers 31, 48, 67
Pesto 27, 51, 73
Pesto Dressing 27, 73
Platt, Courtney 5
Poached Lionfish and Tomato Risotto 48
Potato 26, 32, 41, 50, 52, 57, 72, 74
  Grilled Lionfish with Green Sauce, New Potatoes and Arugula 53
  Lionfish, Beetroot, New Potato and Lambs Lettuce Salad with Horseradish Crème Fraiche 32
  Lionfish Potato Mousse 74
  Lionfish with Chips and Mushy Peas 65
  Lionfish with Sweet Potato Fries, Brussel Sprout Puree, Parmesan Baked Fennel and Lemon Butter 57
  Lionfish with Sweet Potato Toast, Avocado and Cilantro & Lime Crème Fraiche 26
  Pan fried Lionfish & New Potatoes Roasted Sweet Pepper, Fennel with Chili Mint Dressing and Pea Puree 61
  Pan fried Lionfish with Caramelized Onions, Peas and Sweet Potato Fries served with Lemon & Cilantro Mayonnaise 50
  Seared Lionfish on a Spiced Sweet Potato Mash with Soy Sauce and Ginger Dressing 72
  Warm Lionfish and Potato Salad 41
Puree 57, 61, 75

Q

Quesadillas 43
  Lionfish, Black Bean and Mango Quesadillas 43
Quinoa 11, 22
  Lionfish, Quinoa and Chili Omelette with Cilantro 11

Quinoa and Lionfish Solterito 22

R

Red Chilies 18, 31, 33, 44, 54, 55, 66, 68
Red Pepper 18, 44
Ricotta 12
Risotto 48
   Poached Lionfish and Tomato Risotto 48

S

Salad 18, 24, 37, 44, 63, 71
   Lime Marinated Lionfish Salad 20
   Lime marinated Lionfish Salad with Tomatoes, Avocado, Cucumber and Chipotle 25
   Lionfish, Beetroot, New Potato and Lambs Lettuce Salad with Horseradish Crème Fraiche 32
   Lionfish salad with lychee and Chili 18
   Lionfish with Tarka Dal and Cilantro Salad 71
   Thai Style Fish Cakes with Cucumber Salad and Sweet Chili Sauce 44
Salsa 6, 43, 60, 73
Sandwich 36
   Pan-fried Lionfish Sandwich with Pickled Cucumber and Lemon Mayonnaise 36
Sauces 73
Seared Lionfish on a Spiced Sweet Potato Mash with Soy Sauce and Ginger Dressing 72
Shrimp 49, 60
Simple Lionfish Spaghetti 39
Smoked Haddock, Lionfish, Spinach & Bacon Chowder 23
Snacks and Light Meals 34–44, 35–45
Snapper 75
Solterito 22
   Quinoa and Lionfish Solterito 22
Soup 17, 21, 29, 31
   Butternut Squash and Green Chili Soup with Lionfish Ceviche 17
   Lionfish, Chorizo and Chickpea Stew 42
   Lionfish Mexican Chili 54
   Pea and Mint Soup with Crispy Lionfish 29
   Smoked Haddock, Lionfish, Spinach & Bacon Chowder 23
   Thai Vegetable Soup with Lionfish 31
Sourdough 27, 30
Southern Asian Spiced Lionfish with Coconut Rice 56
Soy Sauce and Ginger Dressing 72, 73
Spaghetti 39
   Simple Lionfish Spaghetti 39
Spiced Lionfish Burgers 38
Spicy Lionfish & Snapper Ceviche, Avocado Purée on Tostones 75
Spinach 16, 23, 42, 49, 58, 62
Spring Rolls 16
Butternut Squash 6, 17
Sweet Chili Sauce 28, 44, 68, 73
Sweet Potato 26, 50, 57, 72

T

Tabbouleh 12, 13, 73
   Lionfish Frittatas with Tabbouleh 12
Tacos 37
   Lionfish tacos 37
Tartare Sauce 59
Tempura 70
   Lionfish Tempura with Sesame Broccoli and Cauliflower 70
Thai Style Baked Lionfish 66
Thai Style Fish Cakes with Cucumber Salad and Sweet Chili Sauce 44
Thai Vegetable Soup with Lionfish 31
Toast 10, 26, 27
   Lionfish with Sweet Potato Toast, Avocado and Cilantro & Lime Crème Fraiche 26
   Lionfish wrapped in Parma Ham stuffed with Mozzarella on Pesto Toast 27
Tomato Salsa 73
Travis, James 5

U

Ulman, Aylin 2
University, Lionfish 1, 5, 6, 76

W

Walnuts 51
Warm Lionfish and Potato Salad 41
Western Atlantic Basin 11, 68
Wontons 28
   Lionfish Wontons with Sweet Chili and Soy Sauce 28
Wood, Claire 1, 76

www.ingramcontent.com/pod-product-compliance
Lightning Source LLC
Chambersburg PA
CBHW061750290426
44108CB00028B/2940